THE SUNDAY TIMES

Decision Making and Problem Solving Strategies

John Adair

KoganPage

LONDON   PHILADELPHIA   NEW DELHI

Publisher's note
Every possible effort has been made to ensure that the information contained in
this book is accurate at the time of going to press, and the publishers and author
cannot accept responsibility for any errors or omissions, however caused. No
responsibility for loss or damage occasioned to any person acting, or refraining
from action, as a result of the material in this publication can be accepted by the
editor, the publisher or the author.

Previously published by the Institute of Personnel and Development as *Decision
Making and Problem Solving* 1997 and 1999
First published in Great Britain and the United States in 2007 by Kogan Page
Limited as *Decision Making and Problem Solving Strategies*
Reissued 2010
Reprinted 2010

120 Pentonville Road	525 South 4th Street, #241	4737/23 Ansari Road
London N1 9JN	Philadelphia PA 19147	Daryaganj
United Kingdom	USA	New Delhi 110002
www.koganpage.com		India

© John Adair, 1997, 1999, 2007, 2010

ISBN   978 0 7494 5551 4
E-ISBN   978 0 7494 5890 4

The views expressed in this book are those of the author, and are not necessarily
the same as those of Times Newspapers Ltd.

British Library Cataloguing-in-Publication Data

A CIP record for this book is available from the British Library.

Library of Congress Cataloging-in-Publication Data

Adair, John.
    Decision making and problem solving strategies / John Adair. -- 2nd.
ed.
        p. cm.
    Originally published in 2007.
    Includes index
    ISBN 978-0-7494-5551-4 -- ISBN 978-0-7494-5890-4
(ebook)   1. Decision making.   2. Problem solving.   3. Thought and
thinking.   I. Title.   II. Title: Decision making and problem solving
strategies.
    HD30.23.A3 2010
    658.4'03--dc22
                                                      2009031517

Typeset by Jean Cussons Typesetting, Diss, Norfolk
Printed and bound in India by Replika Press Pvt Ltd